The Grounds of an Opinion

THOMAS ROBERT MALTHUS

London 1815

TABLE OF CONTENTS

THE GROUNDS OF AN OPINION

On the Policy of Restricting the Importation of Foreign Corn

The professed object of the Observations on the Corn Laws, which I published in the spring of 1814, was to state with the strictest impartiality the advantages and disadvantages which, in the actual circumstances of our present situation, were likely to attend the measures under consideration, respecting the trade in corn.

A fair review of both sides of the question, without any attempt to conceal the peculiar evils, whether temporary or permanent, which might belong to each, appeared to me of use, not only to assist in forming an enlightened decision on the subject, but particularly to prepare the public for the specific consequences which were to be expected from that decision, on whatever side it might be made. Such a preparation, from some quarter or other, seemed to be necessary, to prevent those just discontents which would naturally have arisen, if the measure adopted had been attended with results very different from those which had been promised by its advocates, or contemplated by the legislature.

With this object in view, it was neither necessary, nor desirable, that I should myself express a decided opinion on the subject. It would hardly, indeed, have been consistent with that character of impartiality, which I wished to give to my statements, and in which I have reason to believe I in some degree succeeded.(1*)

These previous statements, however, having been given, and having, I hope, shewn that the decision, whenever it is made, must be a compromise of contending advantages and disadvantages, I have no objection now to

5

state (without the least reserve), and I can truly say, wit the most complete freedom from all interested motives, the grounds of a deliberate, yet decided, opinion in favour of some restrictions on the importation of foreign corn.

This opinion has been formed, as I wished the readers of the Observations to form their opinions, by looking fairly at the difficulties on both sides of the question; and without vainly expecting to attain unmixed results, determining on which side there is the greatest balance of good with the least alloy of evil. The grounds on which the opinion so formed rests, are partly those which were stated in the Observations, and partly, and indeed mainly, some facts which have occurred during the last year, and which have given, as I think, a decisive weight to the side of restrictions.

These additional facts are

1st, The evidence, which has been laid before Parliament, relating to the effects of the present prices of corn, together with the experience of the present year.

2dly, The improved state of our exchanges, and the fall in the price of bullion. And

3dly, and mainly, the actual laws respecting the exportation of corn lately passed in France.

In the Observations on the corn laws, I endeavoured to shew that, according to the general principles of supply and demand, a considerable fall in the price of corn could not take place, without throwing much poor lad out of cultivation, and effectually preventing, for a considerable time, all further improvements in agriculture, which have for their object an increase of produce.

The general principles, on which I calculated upon these consequences, have been fully confirmed by the evidence brought before the two houses of Parliament; and the effects of a considerable fall in the price of corn, and of the expected continuance of low prices, have shewn themselves in a very severe shock to the cultivation of the country and a great loss of agricultural capital.

Whatever may be said of the peculiar interests and natural partialities of those who were called upon to give evidence upon this occasion, it is impossible not to be convinced, by the whole body of it taken together, that, during the last twenty years, and particularly during the last seven, there has been a great increase of capital laid out upon the land, and a great consequent extension of cultivation and improvement; that the system of spirited improvement and high farming, as it is technically called, has been

6

principally encouraged by the progressive rise of prices owing in a considerable degree, to the difficulties thrown in the way of importation of foreign corn by the war; that the rapid accumulation of capital on the land, which it had occasioned, had so increased our home growth of corn, that, notwithstanding a great increase of population, we had become much less dependent upon foreign supplies for our support; and that the land was still deficient in capital, and would admit of the employment of such an addition to its present amount, as would be competent to the full supply of a greatly increased population: but that the fall of prices, which had lately taken place, and the alarm of a still further fall, from continued importation, had not only checked all progress of improvement, but had already occasioned a considerable loss of agricultural advances; and that a continuation of low prices would, in spite of a diminution of rents, unquestionably destroy a great mass of farming capital all over the country, and essentially diminish its cultivation and produce.

It has been sometimes said, that the losses at present sustained by farmers are merely the natural and necessary consequences of overtrading, and that they must bear them as all other merchants do, who have entered into unsuccessful speculations. But surely the question is not, or at least ought not to be, about the losses and profits of farmers, and the present condition of landholders compared with the past. It may be necessary, perhaps, to make inquiries of this kind, with a view to ulterior objects; but the real question respects the great loss of national wealth, attributed to a change in the spirit of our legislative enactments relating to the admission of foreign corn.

We have certainly no right to accuse our farmers of rash speculation for employing so large a capital in agriculture. The peace, it must be allowed, was most unexpected; and if the war had continued, the actual quantity of capital applied to the land, might have been as necessary to save the country from extreme want in future, as it obviously was in 1812, when, with the price of corn at above six guineas a quarter, we could only import a little more than 100,000 quarters. If, from the very great extension of cultivation, during the four or five preceding years, we had not obtained a very great increase of average produce, the distresses of that year would have assumed a most serious aspect.

There is certainly no one cause which can affect mercantile concerns, at all comparable in the extent of its effects, to the cause now operating upon agricultural capital. Individual losses must have the same distressing consequences in both cases, and they are often more complete, and the fall is greater, in the shocks of commerce. But I doubt, whether in the most extensive mercantile distress that ever took in this country, there was ever one fourth of the property, or one tenth of the number of individuals concerned, when compared with the effects of the present rapid fall of raw produce, combined with the very scanty crop of last year.(2*)

Individual losses of course become national, according as they affect a greater mass of the national capital, and a greater number of individuals; and I think it must be allowed further, that no loss, in proportion to its amount, affects the interest of the nation so deeply, and vitally, and is so difficult to recover, as the loss of agricultural capital and produce.

If it be the intention of the legislature fairly to look at the evils, as well as the good, which belongs to both sides of the question, it must be allowed, that the evidence laid before the two houses of Parliament, and still more particularly the experience of the last year, shew, that the immediate evils which are capable of being remedied by a system of restrictions, are of no inconsiderable magnitude.

2. In the Observations on the corn laws, I gave, as a reason for some delay in coming to a final regulation respecting the price at which foreign corn might be imported, the very uncertain state of the currency. I observed, that three different importation prices would be necessary, according as our currency should either rise to the then price of bullion, should continue at the same nominal value, or should take an intermediate position, founded on a fall in the value of bullion, owing to the discontinuance of an extraordinary demand for it, and a rise in the value of paper, owing to the prospect of a return to payments in specie. In the course of this last year, the state of our exchanges, and the fall in the price of bullion, shew pretty clearly, that the intermediate alteration which, I then contemplated, greater than in the case first mentioned, and less than in the second, is the one which might be adopted with a fair prospect of permanence; and that we should not now proceed under the same uncertainty respecting the currency, which we should have done, if we had adopted a final regulation in the early part of last year.(3*) This intermediate alteration, however, supposes a rise in the value of paper on a return to cash payments, and some general fall of prices quite unconnected with any regulations respecting the corn trade.(4*)

But, if some fall of prices must take place from this cause, and if such a fall can never take place without a considerable check to industry, and discouragement to the accumulation of capital, it certainly does not seem a well-chosen time for the legislature to occasion another fall still greater, by departing at once from a system of restrictions which it had pursued with steadiness during the greatest part of the last century and, after having given up for a short period, had adopted again as its final policy in its two last enactments respecting the trade in corn. Even if it be intended. Finally, to throw open our ports, it might be wise to pass some temporary regulations, in order to prevent the very great shock which must take place, if the two causes here noticed, of the depreciation of commodities, be allowed to produce their full effect by contemporaneous action.

8

3. I stated, in the Observations on the corn laws, that the cheapness and steadiness in the price of corn, which were promised by the advocates of restrictions, were not attainable by the measures they proposed; that it was really impossible for us to grow at home a sufficiency for our own consumption, without keeping up the price of corn considerably above the average of the rest of Europe; and that, while this was the case, as we could never export to any advantage, we should always be liable to the variations of price, occasioned by the glut of a superabundant harvest; in short, that it must be allowed that a free trade in corn would, in all ordinary cases, not only secure a cheaper, but a more steady, supply of grain.

In expressing this distinct opinion on the effects of a free trade in corn, I certainly meant to refer to a trade really free—that is, a trade by which a nation would be entitled to its share of the produce of the commercial world, according to its means of purchasing, whether that produce were plentiful or scanty. In this sense I adhere strictly to the opinion I then gave; but, since that period, an event has occurred which has shewn, in the clearest manner, that it is entirely out of our power, even in time of peace, to obtain a free trade in corn, or an approximation towards it, whatever may be our wishes on the subject.

It has, perhaps, not been sufficiently attended to in general, when the advantages of a free trade in corn have been discussed, that the jealousies and fears of nations, respecting their means of subsistence, will very rarely allow of a free egress of corn, when it is in any degree scarce. Our own statutes, till the very last year, prove these fears with regard to ourselves; and regulations of the same tendency occasionally come in aid of popular clamour in almost all countries of Europe. But the laws respecting the exportation of corn, which have been passed in France during the last year, have brought this subject home to us in the most striking and impressive manner. Our nearest neighbour, possessed of the largest and finest corn country in Europe, and who, owing to a more favourable climate and soil, a more stationary and comparatively less crowded population, and a lighter weight of taxation, can grow corn at less than half our prices, has enacted, that the exportation of corn shall be free till the price rises to about forty nine shillings a quarter,(5*) and that then it shall be entirely cease.(6*)

From the vicinity of France, and the cheapness of its corn in all years of common abundance, it is scarcely possible that our main imports should not come from that quarter as long as our ports are open to receive them. In this first year of open trade, our imports have been such, as to shew, that though the corn of the Baltic cannot seriously depress our prices in an unfavourable season at home, the corn of France may make it fall below a growing price, under the pressure of one of the worst crops that has been known for a long series of years.

I have at present before me an extract from a Rouen paper, containing the prices of corn in fourteen different markets for the first week in October, the average of which appears to be about thirty eight shillings a quarter;(7*) and this was after disturbances had taken place both at Havre and Dieppe, on account of the quantity exported, and the rise of prices which it had occasioned.

It may be said, perhaps, that the last harvest of France has been a very favourable one, and affords no just criterion of its general prices. But, from all that I hear, prices have often been as low during the last ten years. And, an average not exceeding forty shillings a quarter may, I think, be conclusively inferred from the price at which exportation is by law to cease.

At a time when, according to Adam Smith, the growing price in this country was only twenty eight shillings a quarter, and the average price, including years of scarcity, only thirty three shillings, exportation was not prohibited till the price rose to forty eight shillings. It was the intention of the English government, at that time, to encourage agriculture by giving vent to its produce. We may presume that the same motive influenced the government of France in the late act respecting exportation. And it is fair therefore to conclude, that the price of wheat, in common years, is considerably less than the price at which exportation is to cease.

With these prices so near us, and with the consequent power of supplying ourselves with great comparative rapidity, which in the corn trade is a point of the greatest importance, there can be no doubt that, if our ports were open, our principal supplies of grain would come from France; and that, in all years of common plenty in that country, we should import more largely from it than from the Baltic. But from this quarter, which would then become our main and most habitual source of supply, all assistance would be at once cut off, in every season of only moderate scarcity; and we should have to look to other quarters, from which it is an established fact, that large sudden supplies cannot be obtained, not only for our usual imports, and the natural variations which belong to them, but for those which had been suddenly cut off from France, and which our habitually deficient growth had now rendered absolutely necessary.

To open our ports, under these circumstances, is not to obtain a free trade in corn; and, while I should say, without hesitation, that a free trade in corn was calculated to produce steadier prices than the system of restrictions with which it has been compared, I should, with as little hesitation say, that such a trade in corn, as has been described, would be subject to much more distressing and cruel variations, than the most determined system of prohibitions.

Such a species of commerce in grain shakes the foundations, and alters entirely the data on which the general principles of free trade are established. For what do these principles say? They say, and say most justly, that if every nation were to devote itself particularly to those kinds of industry and produce, to which its soil, climate, situation, capital, and skill, were best suited; and were then freely to exchange these products with each other, it would be the most certain and efficacious mode, not only of advancing the wealth and prosperity of the whole body of the commercial republic with the quickest pace, but of giving to each individual nation of the body the full and perfect use of all its resources.

I am very far indeed from meaning to insinuate, that if we cannot have the most perfect freedom of trade, we should have none; or that a great nation must immediately alter its commercial policy, whenever any of the countries with which it deals passes laws inconsistent with the principles of freedom. But I protest most entirely against the doctrine, that we are to pursue our general principles without ever looking to see if they are applicable to the case before us; and that in politics and political economy, we are to go straight forward, as we certainly ought to do in morals, without any reference to the conduct and proceedings of others.

There is no person in the least acquainted with political economy, but must be aware that the advantages resulting from the division of labour, as applicable to nations as well as individuals, depend solely and entirely on the power of exchanging subsequently the products of labour. And no one can hesitate to allow, that it is completely in the power of others to prevent such exchanges, and to destroy entirely the advantages which would otherwise result from the application of individual or national industry, to peculiar and appropriate products.

Let us suppose, for instance, that the inhabitants of the Lowlands of Scotland were to say to the Highlanders, 'We will exchange our corn for your cattle, whenever we have a superfluity; but if our crops in any degree fail, you must not expect to have a single grain': would not the question respecting the policy of the present change, which is taking place in the Highlands, rest entirely upon different grounds? Would it not be perfectly senseless in the Highlanders to think only of those general principles which direct them to employ the soil in the way that is best suited to it? If supplies of corn could not be obtained with some degree of steadiness and certainty from other quarters, would it not be absolutely necessary for them to grow it themselves, however ill adapted to it might be their soil and climate?

The same may be said of all the pasture districts of Great Britain, compared with the surrounding corn countries. If they could only obtain the superfluities of their neighbours, and were entitled to no share of the produce when it was scarce, they could not certainly devote themselves with any degree of safety to their present occupations.

There is, on this account, a grand difference between the freedom of the home trade in corn, and the freedom of the foreign trade. A government of tolerable vigour can make the home trade in corn really free. It can secure to the pasture districts, or the towns that must be fed from a distance, their share of the general produce, whether plentiful or scarce. It can set them quite at rest about the power of exchanging the peculiar products of their own labour for the other products which are necessary to them, and can dispense, therefore, to all its subjects, the inestimable advantages of an unrestricted intercourse.

But it is not in the power of any single nation to secure the freedom of the foreign trade in corn. To accomplish this, the concurrence of many others is necessary; and this concurrence, the fears and jealousies so universally prevalent about the means of subsistence, almost invariably prevent. There is hardly a nation in Europe which does not occasionally exercise the power of stopping entirely, or heavily taxing, its exports of grain, if prohibitions do not form part of its general code of laws.

The question then before us is evidently a special, not a general one. It is not a question between the advantages of a free trade, and a system of restrictions; but between a specific system of restrictions formed by ourselves for the purpose of rendering us, in average years, nearly independent of foreign supplies, and the specific system of restricted importations, which alone it is in our power to obtain under the existing laws of France, and in the actual state of the other countries of the continent.(8*)

In looking, in the first place, at the resources of the country, with a view to an independent supply for an increasing population; and comparing subsequently the advantages of the two systems abovementioned, without overlooking their disadvantages, I have fully made up my mind as to the side on which the balance lies; and am decidedly of opinion, that a system of restrictions so calculated as to keep us, in average years, nearly independent of foreign supplies of corn, will more effectually conduce to the wealth and prosperity of the country, and of by far the greatest mass of the inhabitants, than the opening of our ports for the free admission of foreign corn, in the actual state of Europe.

Of the resources of Great Britain and Ireland for the further growth of corn, by the further application of capital to the land, the evidence laid before parliament furnishes the most ample testimony. But it is not necessary, for this purpose, to recur to evidence that may be considered as partial. All the most intelligent works which have been written on agricultural subjects of late years, agree in the same statements; and they are confirmed beyond a possibility of doubt, when we consider the extraordinary improvements, and prodigious increase of produce that have taken place latterly in some districts, which, in point of natural soil, are not superior to others that are still yielding the most scanty and miserable crops. Most of the light soils of the kingdom might, with adequate capital and skill, be made to equal the improved parts of Norfolk; and the vast tracts of clay lands that are yet in a degraded state almost all over the kingdom, are susceptible of a degree of improvement, which it is by no means easy to fix, but which certainly offers a great prospective increase of produce. There is even a chance (but on this I will not insist) of a diminution in the real price of corn,(9*) owing to the extension of those great improvements, and that great economy and good management of labour, of which we have such intelligent accounts from Scotland.(10*) If these clay lands, by draining, and the plentiful application of lime and other manures, could be so far meliorated in quality as to admit of being worked by two horses and a single man, instead of three or four horses with a man and a boy, what a vast saving of labour and expense would at once be effected, at the same time that the crops would be prodigiously increased! And such an improvement may rationally be expected, from what has really been accomplished in particular districts. In short, if merely the best modes of cultivation, now in use in some parts of Great Britain, were generally extended, and the whole country was brought to a level, in proportion to its natural advantages of soil and situation, by the further accumulation and more equable distribution of capital and skill; the quantity of additional produce would be immense, and would afford the means of subsistence to a very great increase of population.

In some countries possessed of a small territory, and consisting perhaps chiefly of one or two large cities, it never can be made a question, whether or not they should freely import foreign corn. They exist, in fact, by this importation; and being always, in point of population, inconsiderable, they may, in general, rely upon a pretty regular supply. But whether regular or not, they have no choice. Nature has clearly told them, that if they increase in wealth and power to any extent, it can only be by living upon the raw produce of other countries.

It is quite evident that the same alternative is not presented to Great Britain and Ireland, and that the united empire has ample means of increasing in wealth, population, and power, for a very long course of years, without being habitually dependent upon foreign supplies for the means of supporting its inhabitants.

As we have clearly, therefore, our choice between two systems, under either of which we may certainly look forwards to a progressive increase of population and power; it remains for us to consider in which way the greatest portion of wealth and happiness may be steadily secured to the largest mass of the people.

1. And first let us look to the labouring classes of society, as the foundation on which the whole fabric rests; and, from their numbers, unquestionably of the greatest weight, in any estimate of national happiness.

If I were convinced, that to open our ports, would be permanently to improve the condition of the labouring classes of society, I should consider the question as at once determined in favour of such a measure. But I own it appears to me, after the most deliberate attention to the subject, that it will be attended with effects very different from those of improvement. We are very apt to be deceived by names, and to be captivated with the idea of cheapness, without reflecting that the term is merely relative, and that it is very possible for a people to be miserably poor, and some of them starving, in a country where the money price of corn is very low. Of this the histories of Europe and Asia will afford abundant instances.

In considering the condition of the lower classes of society, we must consider only the real exchangeable value of labour; that is, its power of commanding the necessaries, conveniences, and luxuries of life.

I stated in the Observations, and more at large in the Inquiry into rents,(11*) that under the same demand for labour, and the same consequent power of purchasing the means of subsistence, a high money price of corn would give the labourer a very great advantage in the purchase of the conveniences and luxuries of life. The effect of this high money price would not, of course, be so marked among the very poorest of the society, and those who had the largest families; because so very great a part of their earnings must be employed in absolute necessaries. But to all those above the very poorest, the advantage of wages resulting from a price of eighty shillings a quarter for wheat, compared with fifty or sixty, would in the purchase of tea, sugar, cotton, linens, soap, candles, and many other articles, be such as to make their condition decidedly superior.

Nothing could counterbalance this, but a much greater demand for labour; and such an increased demand, in consequence of the opening of our ports, is at best problematical. The check to cultivation has been so sudden and decisive, as already to throw a great number of agricultural labourers out of employment;(12*) and in Ireland this effect has taken place to such a degree, as to threaten the most distressing, and even alarming, consequences. The farmers, in some districts, have entirely lost the little capital they possessed; and, unable to continue in their farms, have deserted them, and left their labourers without the means of employment. In a country, the peculiar defects of which were already a deficiency of capital, and a redundancy of population, such a check to the means of employing labour must be attended with no common distress. In Ireland, it is quite certain, that there are no mercantile capitals ready to take up those persons who are thus thrown out of work, and even in Great Britain the transfer will be slow and difficult.

Our commerce and manufactures, therefore, must increase very considerably before they can restore the demand for labour already lost; for the and a moderate increase beyond this will scarcely make up disadvantage of a low money price of wages.

These wages will finally be determined by the usual money price of corn, and the state of the demand for labour.

There is a difference between what may be called the usual price of corn and the average price, which has not been sufficiently attended to. Let us suppose the common price of corn, for four years out of five, to be about L2 a quarter, and during the fifth year to be L6. The average price of the five years will then be L2 16s.; but the usual price will still be about L2, and it is by this price, and not by the price of a year of scarcity, or even the average including it, that wages are generally regulated.

If the ports were open, the usual price of corn would certainly fall, and probably the average price; but from at has before been said of the existing laws of France, and of the practice among the Baltic nations of raising the tax on their exported corn in proportion to the demand for it, there is every reason to believe, that the fluctuations of price would be much greater. Such would, at least, be my conclusion from theory; and, I think, it has been confirmed by the experience of the last hundred years. During this time, the period of our greatest importations, and of our greatest dependence upon foreign corn, was from 1792 to 1805 inclusive; and certainly in no fourteen years of the whole hundred were the fluctuations of price so great. In 1792 the price was 42s. a quarter; in 1796, 77s.; in 1801, 118s. a quarter; and, in 1803, 56s. Between the year 1792 and 1801 the rise was almost a triple, and in the short period from 1798 to 1803, it rose from 50s. to 118s. and fell again to 56s.(13*)

I would not insist upon this existence as absolutely conclusive, on account of the mixture of accident in all such appeals to facts; but it certainly tends to confirm the probability of those great fluctuations which, according to all general principles, I should expect from the temper and customs of nations, with regard to the egress of corn, when it is scarce; and particularly from the existing laws of that country, which, in all common years, will furnish us with a large proportion of our supplies.

To these causes of temporary fluctuations, during peace, should be added the more durable as well as temporary, fluctuations occasioned by war. Without reference to the danger of excessive scarcity from another combination against us, if we are merely driven back at certain distant intervals upon our own resources, the experience of the present times will teach us not to estimate lightly the convulsion which attends the return, and the evils of such alternations of price.

In the Observations, I mentioned some causes of fluctuations which would attend the system of restrictions; but they are in my opinion inconsiderable, compared with those which have been just referred to.

On the labouring classes, therefore, the effects of opening our ports for the free importation of foreign corn, will be greatly to lower their wages, and to subject them to much greater fluctuations of price. And, in this state of things, it will require a much greater increase in the demand for labour, than there is in any rational ground for expecting, to compensate to the labourer the advantages which he loses in the high money wages of labour, and the steadier and less fluctuating price of corn.

2. Of the next most important class of society, those who live upon the profits of stock, one half probably are farmers, or immediately connected with farmers; and of the property of the other half, not above one fourth is engaged in foreign trade.

Of the farmers it is needless to say anything. It cannot be doubted that they will suffer severely from the opening of the ports. Not that the profits of farming will not recover themselves, after a certain period, and be as great, or perhaps greater, than they were before; but this cannot take place till after a great loss of agricultural capital, or the removal of it into the channels of commerce and manufactures.

Of the commercial and manufacturing part of the society, only those who are directly engaged in foreign trade, will feel the benefit of the importing system. It is of course to be expected, that the foreign trade of the nation will increase considerably. If it do not, indeed, we shall have experienced a very severe loss, without anything like a compensation for it. And if this increase merely equals the loss of produce sustained by agriculture, the quantity of other produce remaining the same, it is quite clear that the country cannot possibly gain by the exchange, at whatever price it may buy or sell. Wealth does not consist in the dearness or cheapness of the usual measure of value, but in the quantity of produce; and to increase effectively this quantity of produce, after the severe check sustained by agriculture, it is necessary that commerce should make a very powerful start.

In the actual state of Europe and the prevailing jealousy of our manufactures, such a start seems quite doubtful; and it is by no means impossible that we shall be obliged to pay for our foreign corn, by importing less of other commodities, as well as by exporting more of our manufactures.

It may be said, perhaps, that a fall in the price of our corn and labour, affords the only chance to our manufacturers of retaining possession of the foreign markets; and that though the produce of the country may not be increased by the fall in the price of corn, such a fall is necessary to prevent a positive diminution of it. There is some weight undoubtedly in this argument. But if we look at the probable effects of returning peace to Europe, it is impossible to suppose that, even with a considerable diminution in the price of labour, we should not lose some markets on the continent, for those manufactures in which we have no peculiar advantage; while we have every reason to believe that in others, where our colonies, our navigation, our long credits, our coals, and our mines come in question, as well as our skill and capital, we shall retain our trade in spite of high wages. Under these circumstances, it seems peculiarly advisable to maintain unimpaired, if possible, the home market, and not to lose the demand occasioned by so much of the rents of land, and of the profits and capital of farmers, as must necessarily be destroyed by the check to our home produce.

But in whatever way the country may be affected by the change, we must suppose that those who are immediately engaged in foreign trade will benefit by it. As those, however, form but a very small portion of the class of persons living on the profits of stock, in point of number, and not probably above a seventh or eighth in point of property, their interests cannot be allowed to weigh against the interests of so very large a majority.

With regard to this great majority, it is impossible that they should not feel very widely and severely the diminution of their nominal capital by the fall of prices. We know the magic effect upon industry of a rise of prices. It has been noticed by Hume, and witnessed by every person who has attended to subjects of this kind. And the effects of a fall are proportionately depressing. Even the foreign trade will not escape its influence, though here it may be counterbalanced by a real increase of demand. But, in the internal trade, not only will the full effect of this deadening weight be experienced, but there is reason to fear that it may be accompanied with an actual diminution of home demand. There may be the same or even a greater quantity of corn consumed in the country, but a smaller quantity of manufactures and colonial produce; and our foreign corn may be purchased in part by commodities which were before consumed at home. In this case, the whole of the internal trade must severely suffer, and the wealth and enjoyments of the country be decidedly diminished. The quantity of a country's exports is a very uncertain criterion of its wealth. The quantity of produce permanently consumed at home is, perhaps, the most certain criterion of wealth to which we can refer.

Already, in all the country towns, this diminution of demand has been felt in a very great degree; and the surrounding farmers, who chiefly support them, are quite unable to make their accustomed purchases. If the home produce of grain be considerably diminished by the opening of our ports, of which there can be no doubt, these effects in the agricultural countries must be permanent, though not to the same extent as at present. And even if the manufacturing towns should ultimately increase, in proportion to the losses of the country, of which there is great reason to doubt, the transfer of wealth and population will be slow, painful, and unfavourable to happiness.

3. Of the class of landholders, it may be truly said, that though they do not so actively contribute to the production of wealth, as either of the classes just noticed, there is no class in society whose interests are more nearly and intimately connected with the prosperity of the state.

Some persons have been of opinion, and Adam Smith himself among others, that a rise or fall of the price of corn does not really affect the interests of the landholders; but both theory and experience prove the contrary; and shew, that, under all common circumstances, a fall of price must be attended with a diminution of produce, and that a diminution of produce will naturally be attended with a diminution of rent.(14*)

Of the effect, therefore, of opening the ports, in diminishing both the real and nominal rents of the landlords, there can be no doubt; and we must not imagine that the interest of a body of men, so circumstanced as the landlords, can materially suffer without affecting the interests of the state.

It has been justly observed by Adam Smith, that 'no equal quantity of productive labour employed in manufactures can ever occasion so great a reproduction as in agriculture.' If we suppose the rents of land taken throughout the kingdom to be one fourth of the gross produce, it is evident, that to purchase the same value of raw produce by means of manufactures, would require one third more capital. Every five thousand pounds laid out on the land, not only repays the usual profits of stock, but generates an additional value, which goes to the landlord. And this additional value is not a mere benefit to a particular individual, or set of individuals, but affords the most steady home demand for the manufactures of the country, the most effective fund for its financial support, and the largest disposable force for its army and navy. It is true, that the last additions to the agricultural produce of an improving country are not attended with a large proportion of rent;(15*) and it is precisely this circumstance that may make it answer to a rich country to import some of its corn, if it can be secure of obtaining an equable supply. But in all cases the importation of foreign corn must fail to answer nationally, if it is not so much cheaper than the corn that can be grown at home, as to equal both the profits and the rent of the grain which it displaces.

If two capitals of ten thousand pounds each, be employed, one in manufactures, and the other in the improvement of the land, with the usual profits, and withdrawn in twenty years, the one employed in manufactures will leave nothing behind it, while the one employed on the land will probably leave a rent of no inconsiderable value.

These considerations, which are not often attended to, if they do not affect the ordinary question of a free trade in corn, must at least be allowed to have weight, when the policy of such a trade is, from peculiarity of situation and circumstances, rendered doubtful.

4. We now come to a class of society, who will unquestionably be benefited by the opening of our ports. These are the stockholders, and those who live upon fixed salaries.(16*) They are not only, however, small in number, compared with those who will be affected in a different manner; but their interests are not so closely interwoven with the welfare of the state, as the classes already considered, particularly the labouring classes, and the landlords.

In the Observations, I remarked, that it was 'an error of the most serious magnitude to suppose that any natural or artificial causes, which should raise or lower the values of corn or silver, might be considered as matters of indifference; and that, practically, no material change could take place in the value of either, without producing both temporary and lasting effects, which have a most powerful influence on the distribution of property.'

In fact, it is perfectly impossible to suppose that, in any change in the measure of value, which ever did, or ever can take place practically, all articles, both foreign and domestic, and all incomes, from whatever source derived, should arrange themselves precisely in the same relative proportions as before. And if they do not, it is quite obvious, that such a change may occasion the most marked differences in the command possessed by individuals and classes of individuals over the produce and wealth of the country. Sometimes the changes of this kind that actually take place, are favourable to the industrious classes of society, and sometimes unfavourable.

It can scarcely be doubted, that one of the main causes, which has enabled us hitherto to support, with almost undiminished resources, the prodigious weight of debt which has been accumulated during the last twenty years, is the continued depreciation of the measure in which it has been estimated, and the great stimulus to industry, and power of accumulation, which have been given to the industrious classes of society by the progressive rise of prices. As far as this was occasioned by excessive issues of paper, the stockholder was unjustly treated, and the industrious classes of society benefited unfairly at his expense. But, on the other hand, if the price of corn were now to fall to 50 shillings a quarter, and labour and other commodities nearly in proportion, there can be no doubt that the stockholder would be benefited unfairly at the expense of the industrious classes of society, and consequently at the expense of the wealth and prosperity of the whole country.

During the twenty years, beginning with 1794 and ending with 1813, the average price of British corn per quarter was about eighty-three shillings; during the ten years ending with 1813, ninety-two shillings; and during the last five years of the twenty, one hundred and eight shillings. In the course of these twenty years, the government borrowed near five hundred millions of real capital, for which on a rough average, exclusive of the sinking fund, it engaged to pay about five per cent. But if corn should fall to fifty shillings a quarter, and other commodities in proportion, instead of an interest of about five per cent. the government would really pay an interest of seven, eight, nine, and for the last two hundred millions, ten per cent.

To this extraordinary generosity towards the stockholders, I should be disposed to make no kind of objection, if it were not necessary to consider by whom it is to be paid; and a moment's reflection will shew us, that it can only be paid by the industrious classes of society and the landlords, that is, by all those whose nominal incomes will vary with the variations in the measure of value. The nominal revenues of this part of the society, compared with the average of the last five years, will be diminished one half; and out of this nominally reduced income, they will have to pay the same nominal amount of taxation.

The interest and charges of the national debt, including the sinking fund, are now little short of L40 millions a year; and these L40 millions, if we completely succeed in the reduction of the price of corn and labour, are to be paid in future from a revenue of about half the nominal value of the national income in 1813.

If we consider, with what an increased weight the taxes on tea, sugar, malt, leather, soap, candles, etc., etc. would in this case bear on the labouring classes of society, and what proportion of their incomes all the active, industrious middle orders of the state, as well as the higher orders, must pay in assessed taxes, and the various articles of the customs and excise, the pressure will appear to be absolutely intolerable. Nor would even the ad valorem taxes afford any real relief. The annual fourty millions, must at all events be paid; and if some taxes fail, others must be imposed that will be more productive.

These are considerations sufficient to alarm even the stockholders themselves, indeed, if the measure of value were really to fall, as we have supposed, there is great reason to fear that the country would be absolutely unable to continue the payment of the present interest of the national debt.

I certainly do not think, that by opening our ports to the freest admission of foreign corn, we shall lower the price to fifty shillings a quarter. I have already given my reasons for believing that the fluctuations which in the present state of Europe, a system of importation would bring with it, would be often producing dear years, and throwing us back again upon our internal resources. But still there is no doubt whatever, that a free influx of foreign grain would in all commonly favourable seasons very much lower its price.

Let us suppose it lowered to sixty shillings a quarter, which for periods of three or four years together is not improbable. The difference between a measure of value at 60 compared with 80 (the price at which it is proposed to fix the importation), is 33 1/3 per cent. This percentage upon 40 millions amounts to a very formidable sum. But let us suppose that corn does not effectually regulate the prices of other commodities; and, making allowances on this account, let us take only 25, or even 20 per cent. Twenty per cent. upon 40 millions amounts at once to 8 millions—a sum which ought to go a considerable way towards a peace establishment; but which, in the present case, must go to pay the additional interest of the national debt, occasioned by the change in the measure of value. And even if the price of corn be kept up by restrictions to 80 shillings a quarter, it is certain that the whole of the loans made during the war just terminated, will on an average, be paid at an interest very much higher than they were contracted for; which increased interest can, of course, only be furnished by the industrious classes of society.

I own it appears to me that the necessary effect of a change in the measure of value on the weight of a large national debt is alone sufficient to make the question fundamentally different from that of a simple question about a free or restricted trade; and, that to consider it merely in this light, and to draw our conclusions accordingly, is to expect the same results from premises which have essentially changed their nature. From this review of the manner in which the different classes of society will be affected by the opening of our ports, I think it appears clearly, that very much the largest mass of the people, and particularly of the industrious orders of the state, will be more injured than benefited by the measure.

I have now stated the grounds on which it appears to me to be wise and politic, in the actual circumstances of the country, to restrain the free importation of foreign corn.

To put some stop to the progressive loss of agricultural capital, which is now taking place, and which it will be by no means easy to recover, it might be advisable to pass a temporary act of restriction, whatever may be the intention of the legislature in future. But, certainly it is much to be wished that as soon as possible, consistently with due deliberation, the permanent policy intended to be adopted with regard to the trade in corn should be finally settled. Already, in the course of little more than a century, three distinct changes in this policy have taken place. The act of William, which gave the bounty, combined with the prohibitory act of Charles II was founded obviously and strikingly upon the principle of encouraging exportation and discouraging importation; the spirit of the regulations adopted in 1773, and acted upon some time before, was nearly the reverse, and encouraged importation and discouraged exportation. Subsequently, as if alarmed at the dependence of the country upon foreign corn, and the fluctuations of price which it had occasioned, the legislature in a feeble act of 1791, and rather a more effective one in 1804, returned again to the policy of restrictions. And if the act of 1804 be left now unaltered, it may be fairly said that a fourth change has taken place; as it is quite certain that, to proceed consistently upon a restrictive system, fresh regulations become absolutely necessary to keep pace with the progressive fall in the value of currency.

Such changes in the spirit of our legislative enactments are much to be deprecated; and with a view to a greater degree of steadiness in future, it is quite necessary that we should be so fully prepared for the consequences which belong to each system, as not to have our determinations shaken by them, when they occur.

If, upon mature deliberation, we determine to open our ports to the free admission of foreign grain, we must not be disturbed at the depressed state, and diminished produce of our home cultivation; we must not be disturbed at our becoming more and more dependent upon other nations for the main support of our population; we must not be disturbed at the greatly increased pressure of the national debt upon the national industry; and we must not be disturbed at the fluctuations of price, occasioned by the very variable supplies, which we shall necessarily receive from France, in the actual state of her laws, or by the difficulty and expense of procuring large, and sudden imports from the Baltic, when our wants are pressing. These consequences may all be distinctly foreseen. Upon all general principles, they belong to the opening of our ports, in the actual state and relations of this country to the other countries of Europe; and though they may be counterbalanced or more than counterbalanced, by other advantages, they cannot, in the nature of things, be avoided.

On the other hand, if, on mature deliberation, we determine steadily to pursue a system of restrictions with regard to the trade in corn, we must not be disturbed at a progressive rise in the price of grain; we must not be disturbed at the necessity of altering, at certain intervals, our restrictive laws according to the state of the currency, and the value of the precious metals; we must not be disturbed at the progressive diminution of fixed incomes; and we must not be disturbed at the occasional loss or diminution of a continental market for some of our least peculiar manufactures, owing to the high price of our labour.(17*) All these disadvantages may be distinctly foreseen. According to all general principles they strictly belong to the system adopted; and, though they may be counterbalanced, and more than counterbalanced, by other greater advantages, they cannot, in the nature of things, be avoided, if we continue to increase in wealth and population.

Those who promise low prices upon the restrictive system, take an erroneous view of the causes which determine the prices of raw produce, and draw an incorrect inference from the experience of the first half of the last century. As I have stated in another place,(18*) a nation which very greatly gets the start of its neighbours in riches, without any peculiar natural facilities for growing corn, must necessarily submit to one of these alternatives—either a very high comparative price of grain, or a very great dependence upon other countries for it.

With regard to the specific mode of regulating the importation of corn, if the restrictive system be adopted, I am not sufficiently acquainted with the details of the subject to be able to speak with confidence. It seems to be generally agreed, that, in the actual state of things, a price of about eighty shillings a quarter(19*) would prevent our cultivation from falling back, and perhaps allow it to be progressive. But, in future, we should endeavour, if possible, to avoid all discussions about the necessity of protecting the British farmer, and securing to him a fair living profit. Such language may perhaps be allowable in a crisis like the present. But certainly the legislature has nothing to do with securing to any classes of its subjects a particular rate of profits in their different trades. This is not the province of a government; and it is unfortunate that any language should be used which may convey such an impression, and make people believe that their rulers ought to listen to the accounts of their gains and losses.

But a government may certainly see sufficient reasons for wishing to secure an independent supply of grain. This is a definite, and may be a desirable, object, of the same nature as the Navigation Act; and it is much to be wished, that this object, and not the interests of farmers and landlords, should be the ostensible, as well as the real, end which we have in view, in all our inquiries and proceedings relating to the trade in corn.

I firmly believe that, in the actual state of Europe, and under the actual circumstances of our present situation, it is our wisest policy to grow our own average supply of corn; and, in so doing, I feel persuaded that the country has ample resources for a great and continued increase of population, of power, of wealth, and of happiness.

NOTES

1. Some of my friends were of different opinions as to the side, towards which my arguments most inclined. This I consider as a tolerably fair proof of impartiality.
2. Mercantile losses are always comparatively partial; but the present losses, occasioned by the unusual combination of low prices, and scanty produce, must inflict a severe blow upon the whole mass of cultivators. There never, perhaps, was known a year more injurious to the interests of agriculture.
3. At the same time, I certainly now very much wish that some regulation had been adopted last year. It would have saved the nation a great loss of agricultural capital, which it will take some time to recover. But it was impossible to foresee such a year as the present—such a combination, as a very bad harvest, and very low prices.
4. I have very little doubt that the value of paper in this country has already risen, norwithstanding the increased issues of the Bank. These increased issues I attribute chiefly to the great failures which have taken place among country banks, and the very great purchases which have been made for the continental markets, and, under these circumstances, increased issues might take place, accompanied even by a rise of value. But the currency has not yet recovered itself. The real exchange, during the last year, must have been greatly in our favour, although the nominal exchange is considerably against us. This shews, incontrovertibly, that our currency is still depreciated, in reference to the bullion currencies of the continent. A part, however, of this depreciation may still be owing to the value of bullion in Europe not having yet fallen to its former level.
5. Calculated at twenty-four livres the pound sterling.
6. It has been supposed by some, that this law cannot, and will not be executed: but I own I see no grounds for such an opinion. It is difficult to execute prohibitions against the exportation of corn, when it is in great

plenty, but not when it is scarce. For ten years before 1757, we had in this country, regularly exported on an average, above 400,000 quarters of wheat, and in that year there was at once an excess of importation. With regard to the alleged impotence of governments in this respect, it appears to me that facts shew their power rather than their weakness. To be convinced of this, it is only necessary to look at the diminished importations from America during the war, and particularly from the Baltic after Bonaparte's decrees. The imports from France and the Baltic in 1810, were by special licences, granted for purposes of revenue. Such licences shewed strength rather than weakness; and might have been refused, if a greater object than revenue had at that time presented itself.

7. The average is 16 francs, 21 centimes, the Hectolitre. The Hectolitre is about 1-20th less than 3 Winchester bushels, which makes the English quarter come to about 38 shillings.

8. It appears from the evidence, that the corn from the Baltic is often very heavily taxed, and that this tax is generally raised in proportion to our necessities. In a scarce year in this country we could never get any considerable quantity of corn from the Baltic, without paying an enormous price for it.

9. By the real growing price of corn I mean the real quantity of labour and capital which has been employed to procure the last additions which have been made to the national produce. In every rich and improving country there is a natural and strong tendency to a constantly increasing price of raw produce, owing to the necessity of employing, progressively, land of an inferior quality. But this tendency may be partially counteracted by great improvements in cultivation, and economy of labour. See this subject treated in An inquiry into the nature and progress of rent, just published.

10. Sir John Sinclair's Account of the Husbandry of Scotland: and the General Report of Scotland.

11. "Inquiry into the Nature and Progress of Rent, and the Principles by which it is regulated."

12. I was not prepared to expect (as I intimated in the Observations) so sudden a fall in the price of labour as has already taken place. This fall has been occasioned, not so much by the low price of corn, as by the sudden stagnation of agricultural work, occasioned by a more sudden check to cultivation than I foresaw.

13. I am strongly disposed to believe, that it is owning to the unwillingness of governments to allow the free egress of their corn, when it is scarce, that nations are practically so little dependent upon each other for corn, as they are found to be. According to all general principles they ought to be more dependent. But the great fluctuations in the price of corn, occasioned by this unwillingness, tend to throw each country back again upon its internal resources. This was remarkably the case with us in 1800 and 1801, when the

very high price, which we paid for foreign corn, gave a prodigious stimulus to our domestic agriculture. A large territorial country, that imports foreign corn, is exposed not infrequently to the fluctuations which belong to this kind of variable dependence, without obtaining the cheapness that ought to accompany a trade in corn really free.

14. See this subject treated in An Inquiry into the Nature and Progress of Rents.

15. Inquiry into the Nature and Progress of Rent.

16. It is to this class of persons that I consider myself as chiefly belonging. Much the greatest part of my income is derived from a fixed salary and the interest of money in the funds.

17. It often happens that the high prices of a particular country may diminish the quantity of its exports without diminishing the value of their amount abroad; in which case its foreign trade is peculiarly advantageous, as it purchases the same amount of foreign commodities at a much less expense of labour and capital.

18. Inquiry into the Nature and Progress of Rent.

19. This price seems to be pretty fairly consistent with the idea of getting rid of that part of our high prices which belongs to excessive issues of paper, and retaining only that part which belongs to great wealth, combined with a system of restrictions.

www.ingramcontent.com/pod-product-compliance
Lightning Source LLC
Chambersburg PA
CBHW070759180526
45168CB00004B/1682